Dedicated to Imani and Olivia Brown. I love y'all.

God is a Girl Dad. You didn't know? He created the world and placed you in it to grow.

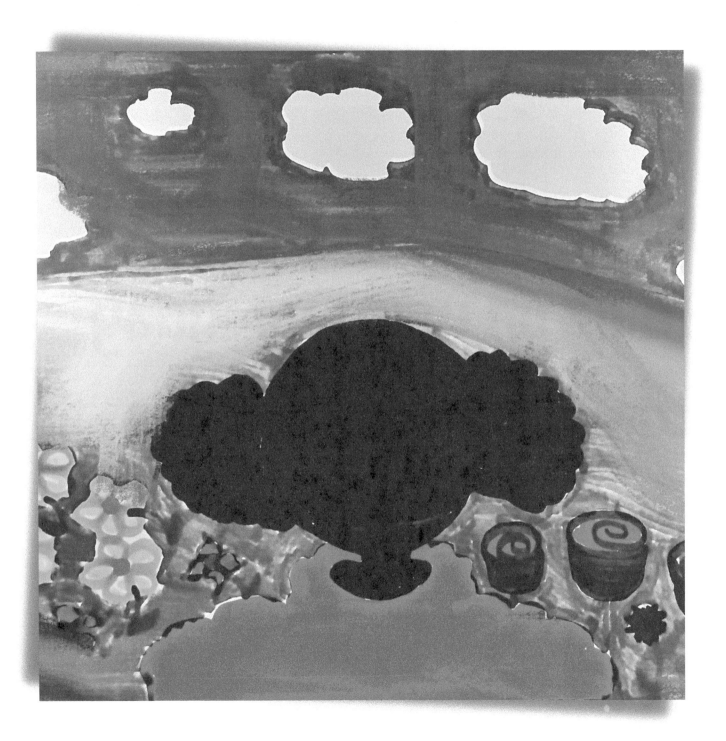

God made the sun to shine on you. Everyday that it rises is a fresh start too!

God gave you a home for you and your family to be safe. You can welcome friends into this place.

God made parties for you to dance and have fun. When it's time to celebrate, you can invite anyone!

A little rain and sunshine can make a rainbow appear. It's God's way of showing you, His promises are near.

God made you a girl. This is true. He knew you would be amazing, beautiful and uniquely you!

YOU

Are

Loved

By God.

The End